YOU ARE

Captivating

CELEBRATING A MOTHER'S HEART

STASI
ELDREDGE

Published by
THOMAS NELSON
Since 1798

www.thomasnelson.com

Published in Nashville, Tennessee, by Thomas Nelson, Inc.

Published in association with Yates & Yates, LLP, Attorneys and Counselors, Orange, California.

Thomas Nelson, Inc. titles may be purchased in bulk for educational, business, fund-raising, or sales promotional use. For information, please e-mail SpecialMarkets@ThomasNelson.com.

Unless otherwise noted, Scripture quotations are from the Holy Bible: New International Version®. Copyright © 1973, 1978, 1984 by International Bible Society. Used by permission of Zondervan. All rights reserved.

Scripture quotations noted NASB are from the New American Standard Bible®, Copyright © 1960, 1962, 1963, 1968, 1971, 1973, 1975, 1977, 1995 by The Lockman Foundation. Used by permission.

Library of Congress Cataloging-in-Publication Data

Eldredge, Stasi.
  You are captivating : celebrating a mother's heart / Stasi Eldredge.
    p. cm.
  ISBN-13: 978-0-7852-8866-4 (pbk.)
  ISBN-10: 0-7852-8866-X (pbk.)
  1. Motherhood—Religious aspects—Christianity. 2. Mothers—Religious life. I. Title.
BV4529.18.E43 2007
248.8'431—dc22

                                2006035098

Printed in the United States of America
07 08 09 10 11 OPM 5 4 3 2 1

For Mom, with love.

CONTENTS

MOTHERHOOD: A HIGH AND HOLY CALLING

I was a really, really big pregnant lady. What I mean is, I was enormous. When I was barely six months pregnant with our first son, I was asked, "Are you carrying *twins*? Are you due any *day*?" Back-to-back questions from shocked strangers. What is it about being a pregnant lady that makes you fair game to *anyone*? And you could tell I was pregnant from every angle. I wasn't a demure pregnant lady who—from behind—looks like every other woman. No, you could tell I was

pregnant from a mile away. By how I looked. By how I waddled.

Anyway, what I want you to understand is that during my pregnancy, my body grew, stretched, became . . . quite large.

Even my feet grew. In my eighth month while out shoe shopping with my own mother, I hurriedly escaped from the store after she asked the salesman, "Do you carry big shoes? Really, *really big* shoes?"

Yes, my body changed. But even as my stomach grew beyond comprehensible proportions, there was another kind of stretching going on—a deeper, slower, more substantial enlargement. My heart was getting bigger, as well.

My heart began to grow with the first flutter of joy at the prospect of becoming a mother. It increased when I felt the first butterfly movements inside my body that the book I was reading said was my unborn child. It grew when I felt my first substantial kick, and it continued to grow as my husband

and I watched our baby do aerobics inside my belly.

Becoming a mother is an amazing thing. Just ask a woman to tell you her birth story or her adoption story, and she will gladly do so with the same zeal as a soldier recounting a victorious battle. When I held my son for the first time, when he nursed at my breast, when I traced his cowlick with my fingers, I felt a stirring in the depths of my soul. It shocked me. I hadn't been this moved since I first surrendered and invited Jesus to come and take his rightful place in my heart as my King. I loved my husband passionately . . . but *this*! This was altogether different. This fierce, abandoned, protective, devoted love was wholly new and profound. I had become a mother. Everything in the world changed.

Now, not only had my body grown, but my heart had expanded to the point that it no longer fit inside me. It now took the form of an eight-pound mystery that was intensely

vulnerable and demanding and hard to figure out. Those first few weeks were tenuous, scary.

What am I saying? It's still tenuous and scary. My heart is out and about, walking around in three young men in a world that is beautiful and fallen, wonderful and dangerous.

Motherhood is a hard thing. As time passes, our babies are born and leave the safety of our wombs; they crawl and walk and then run *away* from us. In fact, a good mother is working toward the day when her son or daughter will healthily and happily live completely independent of her.

The joy of being a mother is so very closely linked with the sorrow of being a mother. It is holy ground.

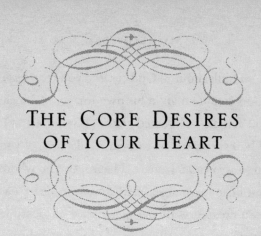

THE CORE DESIRES
OF YOUR HEART

The Scriptures tell us the heart is central. "Above all else, guard your heart, for it is the wellspring of life" (Proverbs 4:23). Above all else. Why? Because God knows that our heart is core to who we are. It is the source of all creativity, courage, and conviction. It is the fountainhead of our faith, our hope, and of course, our love. This "wellspring of life" within us is the very essence of our existence, the center of our being. Your heart as a woman is the most important thing about you.

Think about it: God created you *as a woman*. "God created man in his own image . . . male and female he created them" (Genesis 1:27). Whatever it means to bear God's image, you do so *as a woman*. Female. That's how and where you bear his image. Your feminine heart has been created with the greatest of all possible dignities—as a reflection of God's own heart. And like God, every woman in her heart of hearts longs for three things:

— *To be romanced*. God longs to be loved and to be pursued as well. He says, "You will seek me and find me when you seek me with all your heart" (Jeremiah 29:13).

— *To play an irreplaceable role in a great adventure*. God longs for us to give him center stage in our lives, to join him in being givers of life in a fallen world.

— *To unveil beauty*. God longs to be seen as inviting and inspiring. King David's deepest longing was to "dwell in the house of

the LORD . . . to gaze upon the beauty of the LORD" (Psalm 27:4).

These three things make a woman come alive. Embracing motherhood deeply touches the core desires of a woman's heart.

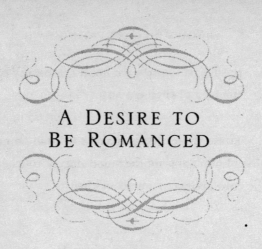

A DESIRE TO
BE ROMANCED

God has been wooing you ever since you were a little girl. The Great Love Story the Scriptures tell us about reveals a Lover who longs for you. The story of your life is the story of the long and passionate pursuit of your heart by the One who knows you best and loves you most.

Indeed, if we will listen, a Sacred Romance calls to us through our heart every moment of our lives. It whispers to us on the wind,

invites us through the laughter of good friends, reaches out to us through the touch of someone we love. We've heard it in our favorite music, sensed it at the birth of our first child, been drawn to it while watching the shimmer of a sunset on the ocean. The Romance is even present in times of great personal suffering: the illness of a child, the loss of a marriage, the death of a friend. Something calls to us through experiences like these and rouses an inconsolable longing deep within our heart, wakening in us a yearning for intimacy, beauty, and adventure.

This longing is the most powerful part of any human personality. It fuels our search for meaning, for wholeness, for a sense of being truly alive. However we may describe this deep desire, it is the most important thing about us, our heart of hearts, the passion of our life. And the voice that calls to us in this

place is none other than the voice of God.

—*The Sacred Romance* by
Brent Curtis and John Eldredge

God has written the Romance not only on our hearts but all over the world around us. God romances us through the laughter of our children, with sand toys and the remembered fragrance of crayons. He pursues us through bath time and fevers and hearts that long for more.

AN IRREPLACEABLE
ROLE TO PLAY

Sometimes, when my children were young, I felt more like a walking napkin than an irreplaceable woman. I call that particular decade of my life "the wiping decade" because I was always wiping something: countertops, faces, bottoms, noses, tears . . . you name it. But a woman doesn't come alive being merely useful. She wants to be needed—essential. She wants to play an irreplaceable role in a heroic adventure.

The world often diminishes the role of

"mother." Moms can feel that their lives tending their children are less noble, less holy, less important than others. But truthfully, the most irreplaceable, essential, powerful, life-impacting role imaginable is being a mother. As G. K. Chesterton wrote,

> To be Queen Elizabeth within a definite area, deciding sales, banquets, labors, and holidays; to be Whitely within a certain area, providing toys, boots, cakes, and books; to be Aristotle within a certain area, teaching morals, manners, theology, and hygiene; I can understand how this might exhaust the mind, but I cannot imagine how it could narrow it. How can it be a large career to tell other people's children about the Rule of Three, and a small career to tell one's own children about the universe? How can it be broad to be the same thing to everyone and narrow to be everything to someone? No, a

woman's function is laborious, but because
it is gigantic, not because it is minute.

—*What's Wrong with the World*

The nurturance of life is a high and holy
calling, and as a mother, it is yours. Oh, may
God open your eyes to see the reality of your
weighty life.

A BEAUTY TO
BE UNVEILED

Every woman longs to be beautiful. But more than an outward beauty that attracts, we long for an internal beauty that captivates; a beauty to the depths of our souls. We long for a beauty that is core to who we really are; we yearn to possess a beauty that nourishes, inspires, brings life. We want a beauty that can be seen, yes, but more, a beauty that can be felt; a beauty that is weighty, that affects others, that is all our own to unveil.

A mother brings beauty to her children's

world through her smiles and her creativity and her tenderness and her compassion to see the needs of others. She births beauty in her children by drawing them to God and by enjoying them, loving them for who they are in the moment.

Jesus says, "I will quiet you with my love" (Zephaniah 3:17, author paraphrase). A woman of true beauty is a woman who—in the depths of her soul—is at rest; trusting God because she has come to know him to be worthy of her trust. She exudes a sense of calm, a sense of rest, and invites those around her to rest as well. She speaks comfort; she assures her listeners that all is well, that all will be well. *A woman of true beauty offers others the grace to be and the room to become.* In her presence, one can release the tight sigh that so often grips our hearts, and breathe in the truth that God loves us and he is good.

Motherhood is a life of sacrifice lived in the service of love. And what could be more beautiful than that?

God Sees the Good
That Is Hidden

A woman's life, lived in intimate partnership with God, is a beautiful thing to behold. Often, however, the only one who seems to be doing the "beholding" is God himself.

Whether we work full-time outside of the home, full-time within the home, or some creative gymnastic combination of both, so much of our lives as women is lived in secret; hidden from the eyes of the world and the accolades of others. So much of it feels mundane. You

don't get an award for doing your 100,000th load of laundry. My family expects to eat dinner—*every night*! So much of what we do feels thankless, unappreciated, unseen. But God sees. And he esteems most what is done away from the eyes of others. He *loves* hidden, secret, small places. He does his best work there—in the home, in the womb, and in the heart.

Every choice you make to love, to serve, to offer, to sacrifice, God sees and is so very pleased. You are joining with him in the amazing work of bringing forth life every time you say yes because it is the loving thing to do. When you say yes, even when you want to say no; when it would be so much easier to say no. Every single time we choose to put our children first, before our needs and our wants, before our dreams and our desires, before our rights and what we deserve, a little bit of our selfishness dies and a little more holiness takes root in our hearts. When you cry out to God in the midst of weariness and loneliness and

sorrow for the strength to love, for the wisdom to discipline well, for the grace to respond with patience, for the help to soothe the ache in your heart, he deepens his presence in your soul and changes you ever more into the woman you desire to be; the woman you are becoming— the woman you were created to be.

This mothering we are called to is an amazing honor. God has invited us to join him in the holy work of bringing forth life in others. We get to partner with God in helping our children become who they were born to be!

And this mothering we are called to is not only about the ones we are birthing life in. It is also about God's deep work in our own hearts. You know that already. As a friend recently wrote to me, "Being a mother has brought out the best and the worst in me." You know that it is hard to love. You know that being a mother has exposed your weakness and your selfishness and your bent toward sin. That's okay. In fact, that's even good. Seeing it is the

first step toward being freed of it! How will we cry out to Jesus in repentance, in need of his grace and forgiveness and life if we aren't aware of our need for him? Dear ones, he knows and he understands and he will be enough. In the midst of our laundry and lists, our carpools and craziness, our meetings and making lunches, God is bringing forth life in *us*.

MOTHERHOOD COSTS YOU GREATLY

It is one thing to suffer. It is something far worse to walk alongside one you love who is suffering intensely and be unable to do anything about it. Many of you have lived this. You know. When I was six years old, I nearly cut my finger off in a slamming door. When the doctor was shooting the painkiller directly into my wound, I looked up at my mother through my streaming tears and heard her say that it was hurting her far worse than it was hurting me. I didn't understand her then, but I do now.

Mothers love and long for their children. Their hearts ache for them, over them. A woman bleeds when she gives birth, but that is only the beginning of the bleeding. Her heart—enlarged by all she endures with and through her child's life, all she prays and works and hopes for on her child's behalf—bleeds too.

A girlfriend of mine is in tears now over the heartache her teenage son is enduring. He is in love for the first time in his life, and the young woman has just broken up with him. His heart is broken. And so is his mother's.

Another girlfriend has been battling stage three breast cancer over this past year. She has endured much. And so has her mother.

When a daughter is found crying herself to sleep over her lack of a true friend, a mother's heart aches. When the doctor turns to the mom after what was to be a casual well check-up of her baby and says, "There's a problem," a mother's heart breaks.

We long to protect our children from the pain and atrocities of this world and although we can do much, we *cannot* do all. When our children suffer or make bad choices . . . oh, how our hearts bleed and ache and enlarge. And that's where Jesus comes in. Now, there is more room for him.

My mother was diagnosed with stage four cancer six years ago and during her illness, while I was visiting to take care of her, she looked at me and tenderly said, "I'm sorry. I'm sorry to be putting *you* through this." There she was, suffering, dying, in pain, unable to eat or even swallow, and she was sorry for *me*; she was sorry to be the cause of suffering in my heart. She would gladly have borne it herself and spared me the sorrow; spared me the pain of bearing her pain, her loss. That amazing kind of concern flows out of a mother's heart, one that has been enlarged by love and by suffering.

A mother's heart is a vast and glorious thing. My mother's heart was expansive, hav-

ing been enlarged by suffering and years of clinging to Jesus while being misunderstood, dismissed, and judged by those she loved most. Me included. It had cost her to love, had cost her much to mother. It always does. But she would tell you that it's worth it; that there is no other way.

I was having coffee with the mother of a friend of mine who was in town to take care of her grandson while my friend enjoyed a little getaway with her husband. The mother was gently lamenting the fact that she lives so far away from her daughter and grandson; she cannot see them as often as she would like. She cannot comfort her daughter, baby-sit for her, hold her when it is all too much. We agreed that this was a sad state of affairs because, as she said, "No one loves you like your mother."

And even as I write those words, I am sadly aware that in this fallen world we live in, many of us were not loved in the way that we

should have been. Not all of us were loved well by our mothers, and a few of us were not loved at all. I am so sorry. Still, it is not too late. Not too late to receive the love, the affection, the healing, and the deep knowing that you were wanted, planned on, delighted in by the One who knows you best and loves you most. Bring your heart to God. Ask him to come for you afresh in this place; this place that deep within still longs to be loved by a mother.

Once you are a mother, you remain one, no matter how old your children become. A young woman who gave birth to her first daughter had her mother come take care of her and the home while she tended her new baby. That first night at home, the little infant made all kinds of mysterious sounds that kept the new mother up all night. In the morning, she was going to ask her mom how long it was before you stopped hearing every little sound your baby made. But before she could ask her mom the question, her mother asked her, "Are

you getting a cold, honey? I thought I heard you coughing last night."

Once a mother, always a mother.

Back at coffee, my girlfriend's mother asked me if my own mother was living, and I had to answer no. My mom passed away five years ago. This dear woman had also lost her mother and it was good to be quiet together, to be still in the knowing that we miss our mothers and that we will miss them until the day we die.

My mother was not a perfect woman. She did not always love me unconditionally, wisely, and well. But she loved me as only a mother can. She loved me from the depths of her enlarged heart. And no one loves you like your mother.

So many times in our lives as mothers, we will have difficult choices to make. Will we stay home from our looked-forward-to weekly Bible study and care for our sick child, or will we wipe her nose really well, hope for the best,

and go? Will we choose to put our son in front of yet another sing-along video, or will we lay down our desired project and engage him in creative play? Will we get the cookies baked in time and keep our kitchen somewhat under control, or will we make them *with* our children and get flour everywhere?

The more we lay down our lives and our control . . . the more true life we will offer and receive.

It is difficult to love. I know! We won't always choose well. I certainly don't. And dear heart, there is grace for us! But so often, someone will have to pay the cost to love . . . either in loving or in not being loved. Sometimes we need to lay aside our time, our days, even our careers for a season so that our children will receive from us what they so desperately need—*ourselves*! And yes, it is hard to do. It is hard when they are young and it remains hard when they are older. It is so difficult to have confronting, serious conversations with

our teenagers. It costs us to engage them on painful issues. But in our relationships with our children, when someone has to pay, when someone has to lay their life down . . . let it be us. Not our children.

Daughters of Eve, image bearers of a life-giving God, you are called to bring forth life. All of us. In our children, in our relationships, in our homes, and in the Kingdom of God. Yes, it will cost you dearly. Just as it has cost God dearly to love. But he will tell you it is worth it.

OFFERING MERCY

We have our "mother tongue," which is our native language. We have "mother earth" from which all growing things come and "Mother Nature," the unpredictable source of typhoons and tornados. The "mother lode" is the source of riches, and a "mother headache" sends you to bed. The "mother of all storms" is fierce and the "motherland" is the home we left and long for. Mother is the source of life. Mother is powerful. Mother can nurture, and mother can destroy. Depending on our experiences,

the word *mother* can evoke images of a warm, welcoming woman or turn our blood to ice.

Whether good or bad, whether redemptive or destructive, our relationship with our mother affected us to the core, helping to shape us into the women we have become. As Dinah says in *The Red Tent*, "If you want to understand any woman you must first ask about her mother and then listen carefully."

We learn from our mothers what it means to be a woman: what femininity looks like, what it ought to look like, how to live as a woman, and the value of a woman's life. We learn many things from our mothers. We receive many things. But the most important thing we are meant to receive from our mothers—and the most important thing we are to offer as mothers—is *mercy*.

Mercy is kindness, compassion, grace, comfort, favor, forgiveness. Mercy implies compassion that forebears punishing even when justice demands it.

RAISING DAUGHTERS

L et's talk about our daughters. How do we mother them well? Answer their question and offer them mercy. Every little girl is asking a question and it goes something like, "Am I lovely?" or "Do you delight in me?" or "Am I captivating?"

Direct them to God and answer them, "Yes!" In every way you can. Delight in their beauty; in their unique personality. Know them. Play with them. Show them the love of God. Train them. Teach them. All in an atmosphere of mercy.

Discipline, correction, and the wisdom you want to impart will not carry the weight it needs to carry if your relationship is not founded in mercy. Finger wagging has its place. But not first place.

Become a student of your daughter's heart. Watch for her interests, her gifts, her talents. Encourage her. Play with her! Pray for her.

And keep praying for her as she enters adolescence! How was adolescence for you? Those years are often tumultuous and painful. That leaving of girlhood behind and becoming a young woman is *messy*. Hormones rage and often the brunt of the raging lands on the mother! The relationship between the mom and daughter will change. We have to let it. This is one of those seasons where our daughters will be walking away from us in many different ways. We have to let them go. Because in the end, we want them to come back . . . all of their own accord.

Many a good woman makes the desperate

mistake of believing her daughter is a reflection of herself—an extension of herself and therefore the verdict on her as a mother and a woman. She is dumbfounded, disappointed, and sometimes deeply hurt when her "little girl" makes choices wholly foreign to what she, the mother, would have done. The result of a mother entangling the verdict on herself as a woman with her daughter's life is a deep wounding and a further twisting of the relationship. The mother will try to set things right—the daughter will pull away even further to establish her own identity.

Your identity as a mother and as a woman is not based on your children. It is not based on other people's opinion of you. It is solely based on your belonging to the God of the Universe who loves you with an everlasting love. Your Jesus has had you in mind before the foundation of the earth to be wholly his. You are loved beyond telling and only *God* has the right to tell you who you are. And you are *his*.

In adolescence the desire of a girl to please her mother is often overshadowed by her desire to be separate from her. Give her the room to become who she is meant to be. Keep answering her question. She still needs to know, "Do you see me? Am I captivating?"

Umbilical cords stretch. Sometimes they strangle. But from birth, a good mother is training her child to need her less and less. From breast milk to solid food. From being carried to crawling to walking to running—our children move away.

As your daughter becomes a woman, continue answering her question. And respect her. You want your infant daughter to grow from baby to little girl to teenager to young woman to woman to friend. It can be done.

RAISING SONS

Let's talk about mothering sons. How do you mother a son well? Answer his question and offer him mercy. Every boy is asking a question, too, different than a little girl's, but core to his heart. And it goes something like, "Do I have what it takes?" or "Am I strong?" or "Am I a real man?"

Direct him to God and partner with God in answering it, "Yes!"

Boys play hard. Let them. Encourage them. See them. Cheer them on! Play with them. Speak to their masculine heart. "You are

strong!" "You are so brave!" "You are fast!" "You have such a good heart. I am proud of you!"

I was on a hike with our three sons many years ago exploring the terrain of a nearby wilderness area when I complimented my eight-year-old son by saying, "You are such a good boy!" He replied earnestly, "I don't want to be a good boy! I want to be *bazooka boy*!" Right!

Become a student of your son's heart. Watch for his gifts, talents, and interests and encourage them. Play with him. Pray for him!

And then—adolescence. That's where two of my sons are now and it is . . . difficult. Sometimes they drive me nuts. See, emerging masculinity is a very awkward thing. It can appear belligerent, snarky, but it's not meant to be. What it really is, is your son stumbling toward strength.

The answer for mothers with adolescent sons is . . . smile a lot. When they do things that irritate you—and they will—smile. You

may want to come down on them, but what they need from you is mercy.

The other day while I was driving my thirteen-year-old home from school, he said to me, "You're really falling down in the sandwich-making department!"

I laughed.

Then I put him in charge of making sandwiches.

Continue answering his heart's question throughout his adolescence . . . as he continues to move away from you and become a man. Pray for him. Pray for other good men to come into his life. And when he is an adult—continue to pray and continue to tell him who he truly is.

Undoing Damage

When your children are young, keep short accounts. Say you are sorry. You are going to make mistakes with your children. It happens. Sometimes, we lose our tempers. Sometimes, we make bad decisions. Sometimes, we need to apologize. Don't be afraid. Let them see your humility. Let them experience offering forgiveness. It is as good for them as it is for us to practice Colossians 3:13, "Forgive as the Lord forgave you." Young children don't have the maturity to process your relationship. However, as they

become teenagers, then adults, their ability to talk about your relationship with them grows.

If your children are adults, the most powerful question you can ask is: "What was I like to have as a mother?" Can you feel the fear rise up in you at the thought of asking them that? Let me go back and say again—your children are not the verdict on you as a mother or as a woman. They are not the report card on your life. If your search for love and security is still tangled up in your adult children, you will not be able to love them well.

Let's go back to asking them the question, "What was I like to have as a mother?" Sometimes it needs to start with a letter. They may not be ready to talk with you about this in person. Maybe it begins with a phone call. But eventually you want a face-to-face conversation.

Ask your daughters, "Did you think I thought you were beautiful?" Ask your sons, "Did you feel I believed in you? That I thought you have what it takes?" If you are lucky, they will tell you what they really think.

Listen. Ask questions. Let the stories come. Don't defend yourself. Don't explain yourself . . . "Oh honey, that's not what I meant!" or "Those were really hard years . . ." Let the weight of their answers come out. Remember, no one parents perfectly. There is no such thing as a perfect parent, save our Father God. We all make mistakes. Let their stories come. And then, ask for their forgiveness.

Most importantly, demonstrate repentance. Pursue them now. Tell your daughters how beautiful they are. Now. Tell them how proud you are of them. Tell your sons they are strong. It is never too late. Your adult children will always need to hear life-giving words from you.

What I'm really saying is, love them. Love them. 1 Peter 4:8 says, "Love covers a multitude of sins" (NASB). If your children know they are loved, a lot of our major failures as mothers, our sins against them, will not become major wounds.

Love them. It is not too late.

MERCY FOR US

Mothers are meant to show us the merciful face of God. Mercy is what we needed most from our mothers, and it is what our children need most from us. It remains as well, that mercy is what we need to offer ourselves.

So often, I feel like I am failing as a mother. I tend to believe that sorrows in my children's lives are *all* my fault. I think that if I was a better mom, they would be avoiding more of the pain in this life. Somehow, if I had parented them better, they would not struggle with a

lack of true friends, an inability to master algebra, being undisciplined in certain areas of their lives . . . whatever. If only I had loved them better and more wisely. If I had practiced playing catch, they would always be picked first for the team. If I had been better about making them practice the piano, they would be able to express their artistry and emotions through music and be stars. If I had worked harder at communication, they wouldn't feel angry, disappointed, hurt, and lonely sometimes. But I didn't mother them *better*. And that feels the same as failing.

Do you ever feel like you are failing as a mother? Like you've ruined your children? Like you've so blown it with them that you despair? Of course you do. And it isn't true.

Oh, it is true that we can grow in becoming better mothers. We can always grow in the grace of God and in his strength to love, to offer, to live more truly, more consistently, more authentically. We want to pursue growth

and healing and a deeper relationship with Jesus so that we can love well. But frequently, when I am tormented by thoughts of being a failure as a mother, it is *not* the conviction of God inviting me to repent and live differently. Rather, it is the accusation of our enemy, the devil, causing me to despair and spiral downward in self-contempt and shame. The sentence that so often haunts us, "You are failing your children," is the number one accusation that comes against us as moms.

And in that place where it feels most true, we need to ask Jesus to speak to us. We need him to tell us what *he* thinks of us as a mother. We must give God permission to vanquish the sentences that aren't true and replace them with his take on our lives. And then, we must exercise the faith to believe him.

As we are a mother to our sons and daughters, God is a Father to us. "I will be a Father to you, and you will be my sons and daughters, says the Lord Almighty" (2 Corinthians 6:18).

Your good, true Father loves you and chose you as his own before there was time (Ephesians 1:4). You are in Christ, and your Father has no condemning thoughts toward you whatsoever. Not a one (Romans 8:1).

The next time you are assaulted with the accusation that you are failing as a mother, ask God if it is true. Get in a quiet place and seek him. Ask him what he thinks of you as a mother; what he thinks of you as a woman. Then wait for his answer . . . it will be better than you hoped.

To Those Called to Mother

I briefly want to speak to *all* women here—
not just mothers in the traditional sense of
the word. As powerful as the role of mother
is, the word *mother* is much more powerful when
used as a verb instead of a noun. Now, not all
women are mothers, but as image bearers of
God, all women are uniquely called to mother.

As daughters of Eve, all women are gifted
to help others in our lives become more of who
they truly are—to encourage, nurture, and
mother them toward their true selves. In

doing this, women partner with Christ in the vital mission of bringing forth life. And *all* women are life-givers.

The impact on a life that has been seen and called out is dramatic and eternal. The nurturing of life is a high and holy calling and as a woman, it is yours. Yes, it has many shapes and myriad faces. Yes, men are called to this as well. But this calling makes up part of the very fiber of a woman's soul.

You can mother other people's children. In truth, our world needs you to. My friend Lori's house was the center of activity while her girls were still in school. Their friends loved to hang out at her house. She offered them life. She counseled them. She encouraged them. She mothered them with love and strength. She also baked them fabulous treats. She has played and continues to play a major role in many young women's lives, impacting them for good; calling them forth to become who they are meant to be.

We mother each other when we offer our concern, our care, our comfort. We mother each other when we see a need and rise to meet it, whether the need is a sweater for a friend who is chilly, a meal to a struggling family, or a listening ear to a friend who is hurting.

All women are called to mother. And all women are called to give birth. Women give birth to all kinds of things: to books, to churches, or to ministries. To ideas, to creative expressions, to movements. We birth life in others by inviting them into deeper realms of healing, to deeper walks with God, to deeper intimacy with Jesus. A woman is not less of a woman because she is not a wife or has not physically borne a child. The heart and life of a woman is much more vast than that. All women are made in the image of God in that we bring forth life. When we offer our tender and strong feminine hearts to the world and to those we love, we cannot help but mother them.

NURTURING
YOUR HEART

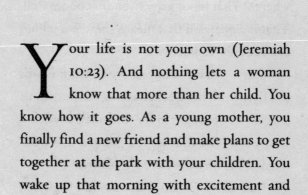

Your life is not your own (Jeremiah 10:23). And nothing lets a woman know that more than her child. You know how it goes. As a young mother, you finally find a new friend and make plans to get together at the park with your children. You wake up that morning with excitement and hope, and your toddler wakes with a fever and the makings for a science project flowing out of her nose.

It truly is amazing how many of our plans,

schedules, dreams, and dates are thwarted by our children. They get older and they forget their homework. They get older still and forget to tell you that Grandma called with an urgent message.

I'm driving home from a soccer game at 7:30 at night with one son when his older brother calls me on my cell phone and asks, "Do we have little plastic farm animals anywhere?" That is not a question that bodes well. That is a question that means there is a school project due. Tomorrow.

Last night, my youngest presented me with the flyer from his teacher asking for nutritious snacks to be brought in for their class breakfast next week. The flyer is, you guessed it, a week old and the breakfast is . . . *tomorrow!*

It happens. On his CD *Deep in the Jungle*, Joe Scruggs sings a fabulous song called "By the Way" about this childhood phenomenon. He sings of a child, who, running late for school, remembers to tell his mother,

> *. . . oh, by the way,*
> *I need an orange juice can,*
> *Four cotton balls, and*
> *Six rubber bands,*
> *And by the way, I'm an angel in the play,*
> *I'm gonna sing and I need some wings.*

Mothers are expected to drop everything and make it happen. And to varying degrees, until our children and we learn better, we do drop everything and make it happen. Our plans for our evenings go by the wayside as we help our son build the mission out of sugar cubes or go over the spelling words or drive worriedly to the emergency room. And do not think for a minute that all of that can be avoided by homeschooling your children. I have been a homeschool mother for more than half of our children's lives. I know. Be as organized as you like, you won't be spared the inconvenience your children will bring to your best-laid plans.

Our lives are *not* our own. This fact will, at times, irritate even the most sainted among us.

It sure has gotten to me. When my boys were young, I was often in utter desperation and at the end of my proverbial rope. I would sometimes give *myself* time outs. Many a mother finds a few minutes' solace by closing herself in the bathroom. I remember well having the flu and being bent over the toilet only to have my three-year-old climbing all over my back. I hadn't learned yet that sometimes it's okay to lock the door! No wonder Susanna Wesley, mother of John and Charles, would throw her apron up over her head in the middle of her kitchen. Her children (she had nineteen!) knew that she was praying and was *not* to be disturbed. You bet her children did not disturb her when that apron covered her face. She had no bathroom door to lock! Can you guess what her prayers were? What have yours been? Often, they are cries from the depths of our heart that go something like, "*Help!*" A prayer right out of the Psalms.

No one said it would be easy. No one ever told us how hard it was going to be either—and if they did, we didn't believe them. And it's a good thing.

Jesus never said it would be easy either. Rather, he tells us in John 16:33, "In this world you will have trouble." He is the master of understatement. He continued to say, "But take heart! I have overcome the world."

Take heart. We need to know more fully what Jesus meant! See, in the midst of losing our lives and what often feels like losing our minds as well, we women tend to lose heart. And that is a dangerous thing to do. In order to nurture and mother well, we must nurture our own hearts as a priority of our lives. Remember, Proverbs 4:23 says, "Above all else, guard your heart, for it is the wellspring of life."

Take time for your heart. What is it you enjoy? What nourishes you? Bubble baths, walks in the park, painting? You may not have much time for it, but you must have at least a

little! Gathering with other women is crucial as well. Bible studies, MOPS groups, Moms in Touch, and book clubs can all provide an arena for friendship and encouragement. Our lives are not meant to be lived alone. We need each other.

Mostly, we need God. We need to cultivate our relationship with him over time with increasing longing and intimacy. God wants us to know him deeply, truly, for as we grow in knowing him, so do we grow in loving him. Because the more we know him, the more we understand how vastly, deeply, and passionately loved *we* are by him . . . right now. Today. In this very moment while you are reading this, your God is absolutely, wildly in love with you! And he wants you to *know* it. Ask him to help you here. He wants to be so very close to you; to live your life *with* you, every moment.

We don't mother alone. We partner with God in mothering—in bringing forth life in

another! While our own hearts drink deeply and rest in God's good heart, he "mothers" us—so that we continue to become ever more truly the women he created us and intends us to be—the women we truly are.

Life-givers.

And utterly captivating.

A Mother's Prayer

Dear Father, thank you for granting me the immense favor of motherhood. Thank you that I am never alone in my mothering, in my loving; you are always with me, every moment. Lord, I give my life to you again today. I am yours. I take my place in your cross and death, your resurrection and life and your ascension and authority. Please fill me with your Holy Spirit and live through me today, Jesus; love through me. Oh Jesus, thank you for coming for me and ransoming me with your own life. Lord, I pray to know your love for me more deeply, more truly, today. Please help me believe what is true. Help me to know you . . . to

know your heart toward me, toward my life. And please fill me with your wisdom and your love that I would live well and love well those you have blessed me with. Please guide me, teach me, and help me to be the mother that I long to be and that my children need me to be.

Come for me today, Jesus. I need you. I love you. I trust you. Help me to love and trust you more. Thank you, God, for loving me. In Jesus' name I pray. Amen.

ABOUT THE AUTHOR

S tasi Eldredge, who is passionate about mentoring women in finding their true identity as the Beloved of Christ, has been leading women's Bible studies for years. With a BA in sociology and formerly on staff with Youth for Christ, Stasi now leads the women's ministry of Ransomed Heart. She has been married to John for nineteen years and has three sons.